MICROSOFT

ACCESS 365

The Complete User Guide for Fast
Understanding of Access 365 for
Beginner and Advanced Users

CHARLES SHERER

TABLE OF CONTENT

INTRODUCTION _____ *6*

CHAPTER ONE _____ *7*

Getting Started with Access _____ *7*

Understanding Database _____ 8

Database tables for storing information _____ 8

Generating a Database File _____ 11

Obtaining the assistance of a template_____ 13

Moving Around the Navigation Pane _____ 14

Designing a database _____ 15

Determining what information you want _____ 15

Separating information into diverse database tables _____ 17

Choosing fields for database tables_____ 18

Deciding on a primary key field for each database table _____ 18

Mapping the relationships between tables _____ 19

CHAPTER TWO _____ *20*

Constructing Your Database Tables _____ *20*

Generating a database table _____ 20

Generating a database table from scratch _____ 20

Importing the database table from another database _____ 23

Obtaining the help of a template _____ 23

Opening and Viewing Tables _____ 24

Entering and Changing Table Fields_____ 25

Everything about data types _____ 27

Designating the primary key field _____ 29

Moving, renaming, and deleting fields _____ 29

CHAPTER THREE _____ *31*

Field Properties for Making Sure That Data Entries Are Precise __ *31*

Field Properties settings_____31

Creating a lookup data-entry list _____34

Creating a drop-down list on your own_____35

Getting list items from a database table _____36

Indexing for Faster Sorts, Searches, and Queries _____37

Indexing a field _____37

Indexing created on more than one field _____37

Dealing with tables in the Relationships window_____39

Falsifying relationships between tables _____40

Editing and Deleting table relationships _____41

*CHAPTER FOUR*_____ *42*

*Entering the Data*_____ *42*

Two Ways to Enter Data _____42

Entering the Data in Datasheet View _____42

Two tricks for entering data quicker _____43

Entering the Data in a form _____43

Creating a form_____44

Entering the data _____46

Discovery of a Missing Record _____46

Finding and Replacing Data _____47

*CHAPTER FIVE*_____ *49*

Sorting and Filtering for Data _____ *49*

Sorting Records in a Database Table _____49

Sorting records _____49

Filtering to discover information _____ 49

Diverse ways to filter a database table _____ 50

Unfiltering a database table _____ 50

Filtering by selection _____ 50

Filtering by form _____ 51

Filtering for input _____ 52

CHAPTER SIX _____ 53

Querying: The fundamentals _____ 53

Creating a new query _____ 53

Viewing queries in Design and Datasheet views_____ 54

Navigating your way around the Query Design window _____ 55

Selecting which database tables to query_____ 56

Selecting which fields to query _____ 57

Sorting the query outcomes or results _____ 58

MOVING FIELD COLUMNS ON THE QUERY GRID _____ 58

Entering criteria for a query_____ 58

Saving and running a query _____ 59

Six kinds of Queries _____ 60

CHAPTER SEVEN _____ 62

*Presenting Data in a Report*_____ 62

Creating a Report _____ 62

Opening and Viewing Reports _____ 63

Fine-tuning a Report _____ 64

*CONCLUSION*_____ 66

INDEX _____ 67

INTRODUCTION

Microsoft Access is a database application management that permits you to keep and manage large collections of data and assist you in recovering them back when it is needed. Until there is an introduction of Microsoft Access certain organization needs may not be acquired.

Microsoft Access is prevailing but Microsoft Access 365 is more prevailing because it is an online version of Access that you can use to keep and manage your data database on the internet.

This user guide is primarily prepared to put you on a plane track and pathway in mastering Access 365, it is a comprehensive practical lesson of total breakthrough from Access 365 tools, this user guide offers you an easy means of learning and a quick understanding of the following Access 365 apparatus and tools:

> ➢ Getting started with Access 365.
> ➢ Create a database file that you will use to save the database information.
> ➢ Working with the Access Navigation pane.
> ➢ Getting started with the construction of the database table.
> ➢ Entering fields into each database table.
> ➢ Entering data directly into the table or employing the help of a Form.
> ➢ Managing tables relationship in the relationship windows for effective database query.
> ➢ Working with the Query Design Window.
> ➢ Format for entering the correct criteria when querying the database for particular information.
> ➢ Creating a specialized report through the query results.
> ➢ Refining the appearance of the Report. And a lot more.

CHAPTER ONE

Getting Started with Access

Access can be irreplaceable for storing and organizing customer lists, addresses, inventories, payment histories, volunteer lists, and donor lists. This chapter presents databases and the concepts behind databases. It displays how to create a database and database tables for storing information. The other aspect of this chapter shows you how to design databases. You need to be aware of database design before you can start dealing with databases. You can just rush in as you always do with the other Office programs.

Access provides a practical database known as Northwind that you can test with as you get to navigate around databases. To unlock this database, kindly follow the steps below.

> Click the File tab.

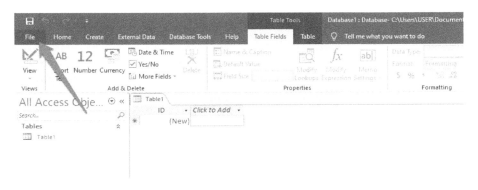

> Choose New.

> ➢ Then in the New window, enter **Northwind** in the Search box.
> ➢ Click the Start Searching button.

Understanding Database

The address book on your computer is a database, so likewise the telephone directory in the desk drawer. A recipe book is also a database, anywhere information is stored systematically can be considered a database. What makes a difference between a computerized database and a conventional database is that storing, manipulating, and finding data is easier in a computerized database.

You need to know how data is stored in a database and how it is extracted, to use database terminology. You must know about objects, Access's bland word for database tables, queries, forms, and all things that make a database a database. These pages provide a crash course in databases. They clarify the different objects—tables, queries, forms, and reports—that make up a database.

Database tables for storing information

Information in databases is stored in database tables like the one in the image below. You include one field for each category of information you want to keep on hand. Fields are the equivalent of columns in a table. The first duty you need to carry out when you create a database is to name the fields and inform Access what kind of information you suggest to store in each field. The database table below is for storing employee information. It has seven fields: ID, First Name, Last Name, E-mail Address, Business Phone, Company, and Job Title.

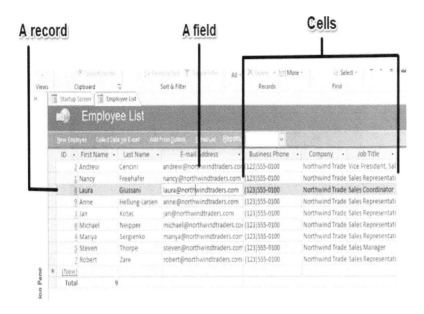

Forms for entering data

You can start entering the records after you create the fields in the database table. A record explains all the data concerning one person or thing. You can enter records directly into a database table, the easiest way to input a record is with a **form.** see the image below:

Fields

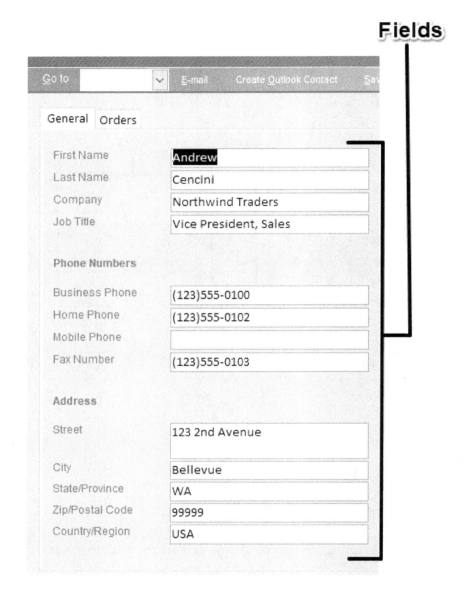

| Go to | | E-mail | Create Outlook Contact | Sa |

General | Orders

First Name	Andrew
Last Name	Cencini
Company	Northwind Traders
Job Title	Vice President, Sales

Phone Numbers

Business Phone	(123)555-0100
Home Phone	(123)555-0102
Mobile Phone	
Fax Number	(123)555-0103

Address

Street	123 2nd Avenue
City	Bellevue
State/Province	WA
Zip/Postal Code	99999
Country/Region	USA

Queries for accomplishing the data out

A query is a question you ask of a database, in an address database you can use a query to discover all the people in a particular ZIP code or state. If information about contributions is kept in the database, you can find out who contributed more than $400 last month. After you create a query, you can save it and run it again.

Reports for offering and inspecting data

Reports can be made from database tables or the results of queries. They are usually read by managers and others who do not get their hands muddy in the database. They are meant to be printed and distributed so that the information can be inspected and examined. Access provides numerous attractive reports.

Macros and modules

Macros and modules are not discussed in this book, but they are also database objects. A macro is a series of commands. You can store macros for running queries and carrying out other Access tasks. A module is a group of Visual Basic procedures and declarations for carrying out tasks in Access.

Generating a Database File
Generating a database is a lot of work, Access provides two ways to create a new database file. You can get the help of a template or do it from scratch. With a template, some of them are done for you. The template comes with manufactured forms, queries, and reports. However, templates are for those who already know their way around databases. You have to know how to change a preexisting database if you want to make use of a template.

Generating a blank database file

Follow the steps below to generate a blank database file:

1. Click the file tab or Access opening screen, then select New.

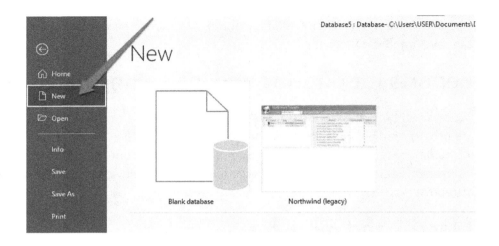

2. Click the Blank Database icon.

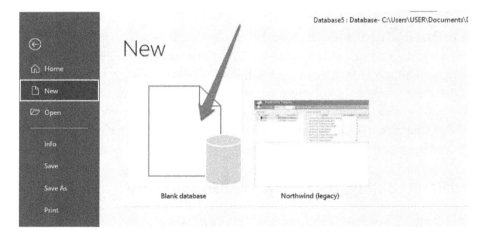

3. Click the Browse button

4. Choose the folder where you want to store the database file, then input a name in the File Name text box, and click OK.
5. Click the Create button.

Obtaining the assistance of a template

To obtain the help of a template, kindly follow these steps to a database from a template:

1. Select New on the File tab, or Access opening screen.
2. Choose a template or use the search box to obtain a template online from Microsoft.

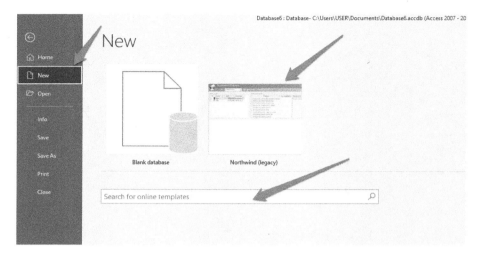

3. Click the Browse button
4. Choose the folder where you want to store the database file, insert a name in the File Name text box, and then click OK.
5. Click the Create button.

Moving Around the Navigation Pane

The first thing that appears when you unlock most database files is called the Navigation pane see the image below:

This is the starting point for carrying out all your work in Access. From here you can choose an object. Tables, queries, and other objects you create are added to the Navigation pane when you create them. Below are the instructions for doing this, that, and other things in the Navigation pane:

> **Selecting an object type:** choose a group (Tables, Queries, Forms, Reports, and so on) from the Object Type drop-down list above the Navigation pane, or choose All Access Objects to view all the groups.

> **Generating a new object:** move to the Create tab and select what type of object you want to create. When generating new forms and reports, click a table or query in the Navigation pane to base the new form or report on a table or query.

> **Unlocking an object:** To unlock a database table, form, report, or query, do one of the following: choose it and press Enter; Double-click it; or right-click it and select Open on the shortcut menu.

> **Unlocking an object in the Design view:** the job of formulating database tables, forms, and queries is done in the Design view. In case an object requires reformulating, right-click it and select Design View on the shortcut menu or click the Design View beneath the screen.

> **Unlocking and closing the Navigation pane:** Click the Shutter Bar Open/Close button above the screen of the Navigation pane (or press F11) when you want to shrink it and get it out of the way. You can also resize this pane by clicking the far-right edge and dragging it right or left.

> **Finding objects:** Use the Search bar to look for objects, The Search bar can be located at the top of the Navigation pane.

Designing a database

To be a database designer is not nearly as fashionable as being a fashion designer, but there are rewards for it. It can be very helpful to you and others if you design your database correctly and carefully. You can enter information precisely. These pages describe all you need to take into consideration when designing a database.

Determining what information you want

The essential question to ask yourself is about the kind of information you want to obtain from the database. Sales information? Customer names and addresses? You can also interview your colleagues to find out what information could be useful to them. Think about it seriously. Your focus is to set up the database so that every piece of information your organization needs can be recorded. The best way to find out what kind of information matters to an organization is to scrutinize the forms that the organization uses to implore or record information.

Plans for database tables and field names

Players
Player Number
First Name
Last Name
Street address
City
State
Zip
Telephone
Email
Team Name
Fee paid
Birthday
Sex
School

Teams
Team Name
Division Number
Sponsor
Team Colors
Practice field
Practice Day
Practice Time

Division
Division Number
Division Name

Coaches
Coach Number
Team Name
First Name
Last Name
Street address
City
State
Zip
Telephone
Email
School

Separating information into diverse database tables

After you have gotten the information you need, you have to think about how to separate the information into database tables. To see how it works, consider the simple database in the table above. The aim of this little database and its four tables is to store information about the players, coaches, and teams in a football league. The Team Name field appears in three tables. It serves as the link among the tables and allows more than one to be queried. By querying individual tables in this database, I can gather team rosters, make a list of coaches and their contact information, list teams by division, place together a mailing list of all players, find out which players have paid their fees, and list players by age group, among other things. This database comprises four tables:

> **Players:** Comprises fields for tracking players' names, addresses, birthdays, which teams they are on, and if they paid their fees.
> **Coaches:** Comprises fields for tracking coaches' names, addresses, and the names of the teams they coach
> **Teams:** Comprises fields for tracking team names and which division each team is in.
> **Divisions:** Comprises fields for tracking division numbers and names.

Determining how many database tables you need and how to separate data across diverse tables is the hardest aspect of designing a database. Below are the basic rules for separating data into diverse tables:

> **Avoid duplicate information:** Do not keep duplicate information in the same database table or duplicate information across diverse tables. By keeping the information in one place. You need to enter it once, and if you have to update it, you can do so in one database table, not numerous.
> **Restrict a table to one subject only:** Each database table should grasp information about one subject only—products, customers, and so on. This way you can preserve data in one table independently from data in another table.

Choosing fields for database tables

Fields are categories of information. Each database table needs at least one field. When you are planning which fields to include in a database table, follow the steps below:

➢ Break down the information into small elements. For instance, instead of a Name field, create a First Name field and a Last Name field.

➢ Give descriptive names to fields so that you know what they are later. A more descriptive name, such as Serial Number, is clearer than SN.

➢ Thing ahead and include a field for each bite of information your organization needs. Including a field in a database table late in the game is an inconvenience. You have to go back to each record, look up the information, and enter it.

➢ Do not put information that can be derived from a calculation. Calculations can be performed as part of a query or be made aspect of a table; this will be discussed in chapter four of this mini-book.

Deciding on a primary key field for each database table

Each database table must have a primary key field. This field, also known as the primary key, is the field in the database table where unique, one-of-a-kind data is kept. Data imputed in this field—a part number, and an employee ID number, must not be the same in each record. If you attempt to enter the same data in the primary key field of two different records, a dialog box warns you not to do that. Primary key fields help Access recognize records and not collect the same information more than once in a query. Primary key fields prevent you from entering duplicate records. They also make queries more effective.

Invoice numbers and serial numbers make good primary key fields. Social security numbers also make excellent primary key fields.

Mapping the relationships between tables

You have to map how the tables relate to one another in case your database includes more than one table. Usually, relationships are formed between the primary key field in one table and the corresponding field in another, named the *foreign key.* See the tables below:

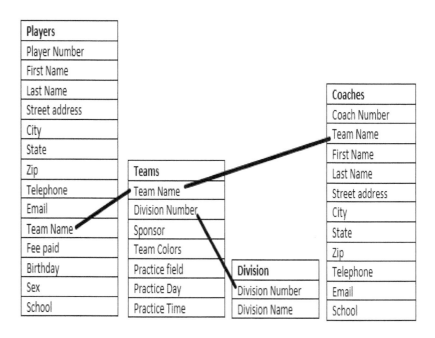

CHAPTER TWO

Constructing Your Database Tables

The building blocks of a database are the database tables. They grasp the raw data. You will have query access and generate reports from several different tables due to the relationships among the tables. This chapter discusses how to create database tables, fields for the tables, and so on, in this chapter, you will discover several tricks and tips for making sure that data is entered correctly in your database.

Generating a database table

The first and most essential aspect of setting up a database is creating the tables and entering the data. Raw data is stored in database tables. Chapter one of this book discusses what database tables are and how to design an impressive one. Access provides three ways to create a database table:

> ➤ **Generate the database table from scratch:** Enter and format the fields one at a time by yourself.
> ➤ **Import the database table from another database:** This method can be a huge timesaver if you can reprocess data that has already been entered in a database table in another Access database.
> ➤ **Obtain the help of a template:** Obtain predesign fields assembled in a table. You can do this if you know Access well and you can change database tables and table fields.

Generating a database table from scratch

Here you create the tables and then enter the fields one after the other. After creating or opening a database file, kindly follow the instructions below to create a database table from scratch:

1. **Visit the Create tab.**

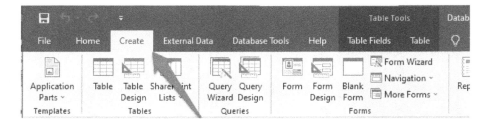

2. **Click the Table Design button.**

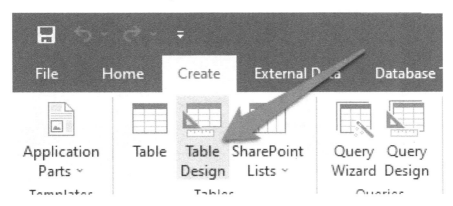

The Design window comes into sight. From here, you enter fields for your database table. See the image below.

3. **Click the Save button on the Quick Access toolbar.**

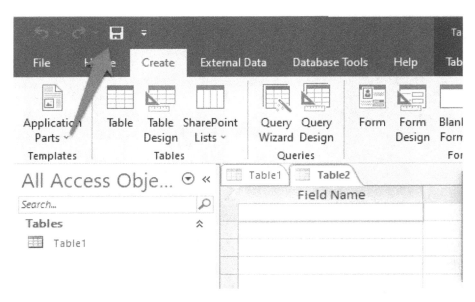

The Save As dialog box appears.

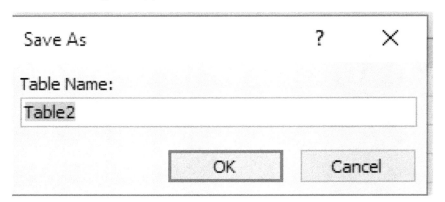

4. **Enter a descriptive name for your table and click ok.** When you go back to the Navigation pane you will see the name of the table you created. In case you do not trust me, click the Tables group to view the names of tables in your database.

Importing the database table from another database

Rare things are more monotonous than entering records in a database table. In case the record you want was already imputed somewhere else, more power to you. Kindly follow these instructions to obtain a database table from another Access database:

1. **Visit the External data tab.**

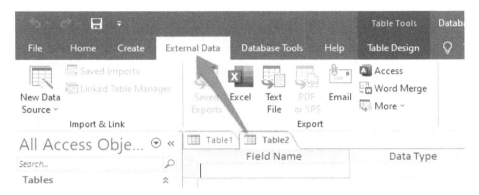

2. **Click the New Data Source button, and in the File Open dialog box, choose the Access database with the table you need and click Open.** The Get External Data-Access Database dialog box unlocks.
3. **Click the Browse Button, and in the File Open dialog box, choose the Access database with the table you need and click Open.** You go back to the Get External Data-Access Database dialog box.
4. **Choose the first option button (Import Tables, Queries, Forms, Reports, Macros, and Modules into the Recent Database) and then click OK.**
5. **Choose the database table you want on the Tables tab.** You can import more than one database table by clicking the Select All button or clicking numerous table names.
6. **Then click OK.**

Obtaining the help of a template

Kindly follow these steps to obtain the help of a template in creating a table (and accompanying queries, reports, and forms):

1. **Close all objects in case any objects are open.** To close an object, click its Close button or right-click its tab and select Close on the shortcut menu.

2. **Click the Application Parts button on the Create tab.** A drop-down menu with options for creating forms and tables comes into sight. (The tables are listed under 'Quick Start').

3. **Select Contacts, Issues, Tasks, or Users.** In case you have other tables in your database, a dialog box asks you if you want to create a relationship between the table you are creating and another table.

4. **Choose the There Is No Relationship option button and click Create.** "Establishing Relationships among Database Tables" explains how to create relationships on your own and this will be explained later in this chapter. But if you want to create these relationships now and you have the means to do it, choose an option besides There is No Relationship, select a table on the drop-down menu, and then click the Next button to select which field to forge the relationship with.

5. **On the Navigation pane, right-click the name of the table you created and select Design View.** In the Design view, you can view the names of the fields in the table.

Opening and Viewing Tables

To unlock a table, start in the Navigation pane and choose the Tables group to see the names of the database tables you created. The way you unlock a table depends on whether you want to open it in the Design view or Datasheet view.

❖ Design view is for creating fields and describing their parameters.
❖ Datasheet view is for entering and examining data in a table.

Pick a table on the Navigation pane and use one of these methods to open and view it:

❖ **Opening in Design View:** Right-click the table's name in the Navigation pane and select Design View on the shortcut menu.

- ❖ **Opening in Datasheet view:** On the Navigation pane, double-click the table's name or right-click its name and select Open on the shortcut menu.
- ❖ **Switching between views by right-clicking:** Right-click the table's tab and select Datasheet View or Design View.
- ❖ **Switching between views on the status bar:** click the Datasheet View or Design View button on the right side of the status bar.
- ❖ **Switching between views with the View button:** On the Home tab, click the View Button and select Datasheet View or Design View.

Entering and Changing Table Fields

The next thing to do after you have created a database table is to enter the fields, and if Access created the table for you, you just need to change the fields to your taste. Fields determine what kind of information is kept in a database table.

Generating a field

You can generate a field on your own or obtain Access's help and create a ready-made field. Both methods are discussed here.

Generating a field on your own

To generate a field on your own, unlock the table that needs a new field and follow the instructions on the (Table Tools) Table Design tab:

1. **Change to design view if you are not already there:** To change to Design view, click the Design View button on the status bar.
2. **Insert a new row for the field, if necessary:** To do this, click in the field that is to go after the new field, then click the insert Rows button on the (Table Tools) Table Design tab.
3. **Enter a name in the Field Name column:** Names can not be longer than 64 letters and they cannot include periods.
4. **Press the Tab key or click in the Data Type column, and select a data type from the drop-down list, as displayed in the image below:**

Define field properties   **Select a data type**

5. **Enter a description in the Description column this is optional:** These descriptions can be very useful when you want to reacquaint yourself with a field and discover what it is meant for.

Taking advantage of ready-made fields

To create a ready-made field, kindly follow the steps below:

❖ **Change to Datasheet view by clicking the datasheet view button.**

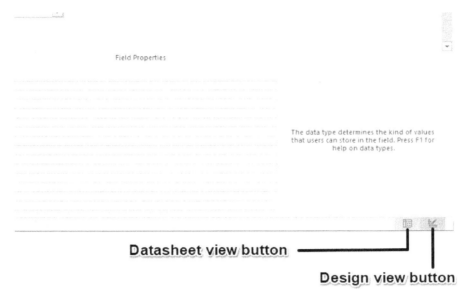

Field Properties

The data type determines the kind of values that users can store in the field. Press F1 for help on data types.

Datasheet view button ——————

Design view button

❖ Choose the field that you want your recent field to go after.
❖ On the (Table Tools) Table Fields tab, click a field button or click the More Fields button and select the name of a field on the drop-down list.

Search for field buttons in the Add & Delete group. Field buttons include Short Text, Currency, and Number. After you create your recent field, change to Design view and examine its field properties. Some of these properties may require changing. See "Field Properties for Making Sure That Data Entries Are Accurate" for information concerning field properties.

Everything about data types

Data types are the first line of defense in making sure that data is imputed accurately in a table, to select a data type for a field, start in Design view, unlock the Data Type drop-down menu, and select a data type. Select data types carefully, because the way you classify the data that is imputed in a field determines how you query the field for information. The table below discusses the options on the Data Type drop-down list.

27

Data Types for Fields

Data Type	What it is meant for
Short Text	For storing text (city names, for instance) combinations of text and numbers (street addresses, for instance) numbers that won't be calculated (telephone numbers, social security numbers, ZIP codes, for instance)
Long Text	For keeping long descriptions.
Number	For keeping numbers to be used in calculations or sorting.
Large Number	For importing and linking to Bright (big integer) data. This data type is for working with calculations involving extremely large numbers
Currency	For keeping monetary figures for use in calculating and storing.
Date/Time	For keeping dates and times and using dates and times in calculations.
Date/Time Extended	For keeping dates and times such that they are compatible with the SQL Server datatime2 data type.
Yes/No	For keeping True/False, Yes/No, and On/off type data.
AutoNumber	For imputing numbers in sequence that will be distinct from record to record. Use this data type for the primary key field.
OLE Object	This is used for embedding an OLE link in your Access table to another object Excel worksheet or Word document.
Calculated	For entering a mathematical expression that uses data from other fields in the database table.

Hyperlink	For keeping hyperlinks to other locations on the internet.
Lookup Wizard	For creating a drop-down list with choices that a data-entry clerk can select from when entering data.
Attachment	This is used for keeping an image, spreadsheet, document, chart, or other file.

Designating the primary key field

Selecting a primary key field is so essential that Access does not let you close a table unless you select one. Follow these instructions on the (Table Tools) Table Design tab to designate a field in a database table as the primary key field:

❖ **In Design view, choose the field or fields you want to be the primary key:** To choose a field, click its row selector, the slight box by its left; Ctrl+click row selectors to choose more than one field.

❖ **Click the Primary Key button:** A slight key symbol displays on the row selector to let you know which field or fields are the primary key fields.

To remove a primary key, click its row selector and then click the Primary Key button all over again.

Moving, renaming, and deleting fields

To move, rename, or delete a field. Change to Design view and kindly follow these steps:

❖ **Moving a field:** Choose the field's row selector and release the mouse button. Then click one more time and drag the selector up or down to a new location.

❖ **Renaming a field:** Click in the Field Name box where the name is, delete the name that is there, and enter a new name.

❖ **Deleting a field:** Click in the Field Name box, visit the (Table Tools) Table Design tab, and click the Delete Rows button. You can also right-click the field and select Delete Rows on the shortcut menu.

CHAPTER THREE

Field Properties for Making Sure That Data Entries Are Precise

People do make mistakes when they enter data in a database table. One way to cut down on mistakes is to take advantage of the Field Properties settings on the General tab in the Design view window.

Field Properties settings

The field properties settings safeguard data from being entered wrongly. Following is a description of the diverse properties and a guide for using them wisely.

Field Size

In the Field Size box for Text Fields, input the maximum number of characters that can be entered in the field. For instance, if the field you are dealing with is a ZIP code, and you need to input six-number ZIP codes. By inputting 6 in the Field Size text box, only six characters can be entered in the field. A sleepy data-entry clerk could not enter a seven-character ZIP code by coincidence.

Format

This has been discussed earlier in this chapter. Click the drop-down list and select the format in which text, numbers, dates, and times are shown.

Decimal Places

For a field that grasps numbers, unlock the Decimal Places drop-down menu and select how many numbers can appear to the right of the decimal point.

Input Mask

This feature offers a template with punctuation marks to make entering the data easier, for Text and Date field types. Social security numbers, Telephone numbers, and other numbers that typically are entered along with dashes and parentheses are ideal candidates for an input mask.

Caption

In case the field you are working on has a cryptic or difficult-to-understand name, impute a more descriptive name in the Caption text box.

Value Default

When you notice that the majority of records require a certain value, number, or abbreviation, enter it in the Default Value text box.

Validation Rule

When you can find your way around operators and Boolean expressions, you can establish a rule for entering data in a field. For instance, you can impute an expression that requires dates to be imputed in a certain time frame. Below are some examples of validation rules:

<800	The value you enter must be less than 800
>800	The value you enter must be above 800
<>0	The value you enter cannot be zero

>=#1/1/2024#	The date you enter must be January 1, 2024, or later.

Validation Text

If someone imputes data that disrupts a validation rule that you impute in the validation Rule text box, Access shows a standard error message.

Required

By evasion, no entry has to be made in a field, but if you select Yes instead of No in the Required box and you fail to make an entry in the field, a message box informs you to be sure to make an entry.

Allow Zero Length

This property permits you to enter zero-length strings in a field. A zero-length string which is indicated by two quotation marks with no text or spaces between them ("") −reveals that no value exists for a field.

Indexed

This property shows whether the field has been indexed. As "Indexing for Faster Sorts, Searches, and Queries" clarifies, later in this chapter, indexes make sorting fields and searching through a field go faster.

Unicode Expression

Select Yes from the Unicode Expression drop-down list if you want to compress data that is now kept in Unicode format, which is a standardized encoding scheme. When you store data in this manner it saves on disk space, and you perhaps don't want to change this property.

Smart Tags

If you want to enter Smart Tags in the field, specify which kind you enter by clicking the three dots next to the Smart Tags box and selecting an option in the Action Tags dialog box.

Text Align

This property regulates how the text is aligned in a column or on a report or form. pick General to let Access determine the alignment, or choose Left, Right, Center, or distribute.

Text Format

This drop-down list lets you select to permit rich text in the field, It is obtainable on the Long Text field. With this property set to Rich Text, you can make diverse words bold, italic, underline, and modify font sizes and colors. Set it to Plain Text for plain, boring text with no formatting.

Append Only

This property lets you add data only to a Long Text field to collect a history of comments, it is obtainable on Long Text fields.

Show Date Picker

This property is obtainable on the Date/Time fields. Select Dates to place a button next to the column that data-entry clerks can click to open a calendar and choose a date instead of typing numbers.

IME Mode/IME Sentence mode

These options are for changing characters and sentences from East Asian versions of Access.

Creating a lookup data-entry list

Conceivably the best way to make sure that data is imputed accurately is to create a data-entry drop-down list. Therefore, anybody entering the data in your database table can do so by selecting an item from the list and not by typing it in, this technique saves time and prevents invalid data from being entered. Access provides two ways to create the drop-down list:

❖ **Create the list by entering the items yourself:** You can take this path when you are dealing with a finite list of items that never change.

❖ **Obtain the items from another database table:** Take this path to get items from a column in another database table. In this manner, you can select from an ever-expanding list of items. This is an amazing way of getting items from a primary key field in another table. When the number of items in the other database changes, so as well the number of items in the drop-down list, because the items come from the other database table.

Creating a drop-down list on your own

Kindly follow these instructions to create a drop-down, or lookup, list with entries you type:

1. **Pick the field that requires a drop-down list, in Design view.**

2. **Unlock the Data Type drop-down list and select Lookup Wizard, the last option in the list.**

   The Lookup Wizard dialog box comes into sight.

3. **Choose the second option, I will type in the Data that I desire, and then click the Next button.**

4. **Underneath Col 1 in the next dialog box, enter each item you want to appear in the drop-down list; then click the Next button.**

   You can generate a multicolumn list by entering a number in the Number of Columns text box and then entering items for the list.

5. **Enter a name for the field, if essential, and click the finish button.**

   Navigate to Datasheet view and unlock the drop-down list in the field to make sure that it shows appropriately.

To eliminate a lookup list from a field, choose the field, visit the Lookup tab in the Design view window, unlock the Display Control drop-down list, and select Text Box. See the Lookup properties in the image below:

Getting list items from a database table

Follow these instructions below to get items in a drop-down list from another database table:

1. **In Design view, click the field that wants a list, unlock the Data Type drop-down list, and select Lookup Wizard.**

   The Lookup Wizard dialog box appears.

2. **Choose the first option, I want the Lookup Field to Get the Values from Another Query or Table. Then click Next.**

   You notice a list of tables in your database.

3. **Choose the table with the data you want and click the Next button.**

   The dialog box displays a list of obtainable fields in the table.

4. **Choose the field where the data for your list is kept.**
5. **Click the > button.**

The names of the lists are displayed on the right-hand side of the dialog box, under Selected Fields.

6. **Click the Next button.**
7. **Then click the Finish button.**

Indexing for Faster Sorts, Searches, and Queries

In a large database table, indexes make sorting, searching, and querying go greatly faster because Access looks through its data rather than the data in tables. Indexing means to instruct Access to keep information about the data in a field or combination of fields.

Indexing a field

To index a field, change to Design view, choose the field you want to index, and on the General tab of the field Properties part of the Design window, unlock the indexed drop-down list and select one of these options:

➢ **Yes (Duplicates OK):** Indexes the field and permits duplicate values to be entered in the field.

➢ **Yes (No Duplicates):** Indexes the field and disallows duplicate values.

Indexing created on more than one field

An index generated on more than one field is known as a multifield index. Multifield indexes make sorting, searching, and querying the database table go faster. Kindly follow the steps below to generate a multifield index:

➢ **Change to Design view, and on the (Table Tools) Table Design tab, click the indexes button.**

You notice the indexes dialog box, as displayed in the image below.

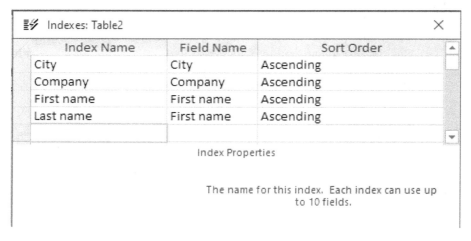

- ➢ **On the blank line in the dialog box, impute a name for the index in the index Name column.**
- ➢ **Unlock the drop-down list and select the first field you want for the multifield index.**

Access sorts the records first on this field and then on the second field you select.

> **In the next row, leave the index Name blank and select another field name from the drop-down menu.**

This field is the second field in the index. You can use as many as ten diverse fields in a multifield index.

> **Select Descending in the Sort Order column in case you want the field sorted in descending order.**

Whenever you want to leave the Sort Order set to Ascending because most people read from A to Z.

> **Click the Close button.**

Dealing with tables in the Relationships window

Unlock the Relationship window to manage database tables and their relationships to each other. To unlock this window, visit the Database Tools tab and click the Relationships button. Access unlocks the (Relationship Tools) Relationship Design tab for you to deal with table relationships.

Before you can create a relationship between tables, you have to position tables in the Relationships Design window. Kindly follow these instructions to add a table to the window:

> **In the (Relationships Tools) Relationships Design tab, select the Add Tables button (You may have to click the Database Tool first).**

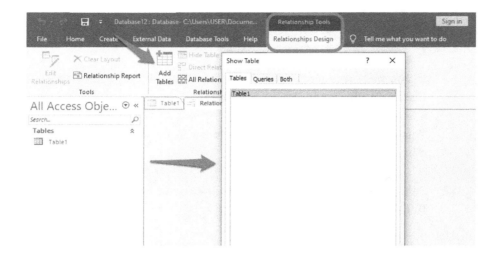

> **Drag a table name from the task pane into the window.**

Falsifying relationships between tables

On the (Relationship Tools) Relationships Design tab, then be certain that both tables are on display and kindly follow these instructions to falsify a relationship between them:

1. **Click to choose the field in one table; then grasp down the mouse button, drag the pointer to the field in the other table where you need to falsify the link, and then release the mouse button.**
2. **Choose the Enforce Referential Integrity check box:** if you do not choose this box, the relationship between the tables is unclassified, instead of being a one-to-many relationship.
3. **Choose Cascade options if you so select**.

   One of these options is amazing; the other is hazardous:

   > **Cascade Update Related Fields:** in case you change a value on the "one" side of the relationship, a matching value on the "many" side changes as well to preserve referential honesty.

> **Cascade Delete Related Records:** if you delete a record in the "one" table, all records in the "many" table to which the deleted record is linked are also deleted.
4. **Click the Create button to falsify the relationship.**

Editing and Deleting table relationships

In the Relationships window, choose the line that signifies the relationship between two database tables and follow these steps to edit or remove the relationship:

❖ **Editing the relationship:** Click the Edit Relationships button, right-click and select Edit Relationships, or double-click the line. The relationship dialog box appears, where you can refit the relationship.

❖ **Deleting the relationship:** Press the Delete key or right-click and select Delete. Then choose Yes in the confirmation box.

CHAPTER FOUR

Entering the Data

Finally, you can now start entering the data. If you have set up your database tables, named your fields, and established relationships between the tables, you are good to go. This chapter describes how to enter the data in a database table it also explains how to find missing records in case one goes off track.

Two Ways to Enter Data

There are two ways to enter data in a database table, they are Database view and a form. here are the benefits of entering data in the Datasheet view:

- ❖ You can compare data easily between records.
- ❖ You can navigate up or down to find records.
- ❖ Many records appear simultaneously.
- ❖ You can sort by column with the commands in the Sort and Filter group on the Home tab.

Below are the advantages of entering the data in a form:

- ❖ Getting from field to field is easier.
- ❖ Fields are clearly labeled so that you always see what to enter.
- ❖ You don't have to navigate left or right to view all the fields.

Entering the Data in Datasheet View

In Datasheet view, the bottommost of the window states how many records are entered in the database table and which record the cursor is in. To enter a new record, go to a new, empty row and begin to enter the data. To create a new row, kindly do one of the following:

- ❖ **On the Home tab, click the New button.**
- ❖ **Click the New (Blank) Record button in the Datasheet navigation buttons.** These buttons can be found beneath the left corner of the Datasheet view window.
- ❖ **Navigate to the bottommost of the Datasheet view window and begin typing in the row with an asterisk (*) next to it.**
- ❖ **Press Ctrl++(the plus key).**

A pencil icon comes into sight on the row selector to let you discover which record you are working with. To navigate from field to field, click in a field, press enter, or press the Tab key.

To delete a record, click its row selector and press the delete key or the Delete button (which can be found on the Home Tab).

Two tricks for entering data quicker

In a database with numerous fields, sometimes it's difficult to tell what data to enter. When the pointer is in the sixth or seventh field, for instance, you can lose sight of the first field, the one on the left side of the datasheet that usually identifies the person or item whose record you are entering.

To freeze a field so that it displays onscreen no matter how you navigate to the right side of the datasheet, right-click the field's column heading and select Freeze Fields on the shortcut menu. To unfreeze the fields, right-click the column heading and select Unfreeze All Fields on the shortcut menu. You can also freeze more than one field by dragging over field names at the topmost of the datasheet before selecting to freeze the columns.

Another way to deal with the issue of not being able to recognize where data is supposed to be entered is to hide columns in the datasheet. To execute this trick, kindly follow the steps below:

> **Choose the columns you want to hide by dragging the pointer across their names.**
> **Right-click the column heading and select Hide Fields on the shortcut menu.**
> **To view the columns one more time, right-click any column heading and select Unhide Fields on the shortcut menu.** The Unhide Columns dialog box appears.
> **Choose the fields that you want to see on the datasheet.**

Entering the Data in a form

Forms like the one displayed below are easier for entering data. The label shows you exactly what to impute.

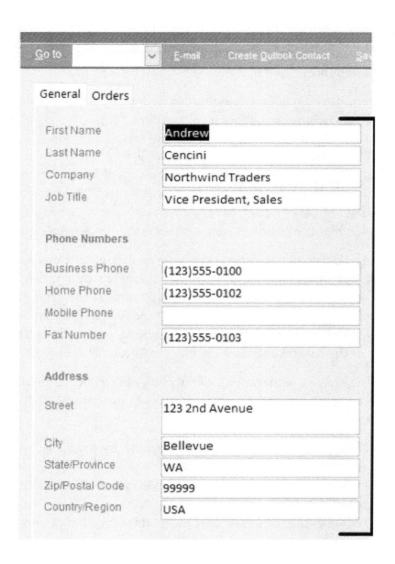

Creating a form

To create a form, visit the Create tab and click the Form Wizard button.

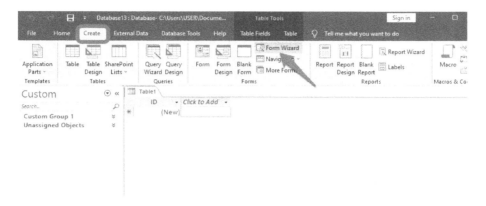

You will see the first of several Form Wizard dialog boxes. Provide an answer to these questions and continue clicking the Next button until the time comes to click Finish:

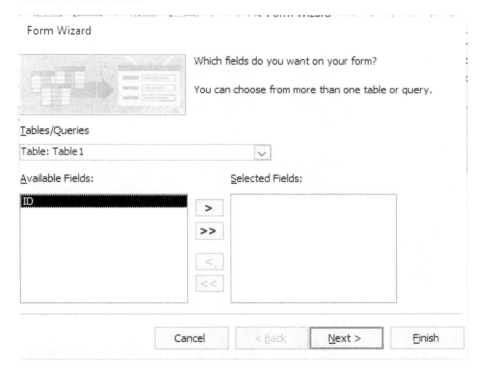

- ❖ **Tables/Queries:** From the drop-down menu, select the name of the database table you want to enter data in.
- ❖ **Selected Fields:** Click the >>button to enter all the field names in the Select Fields box.

❖ **Layout:** Choose the Columnar option button. The other layouts are not very decent for entering data in a table. If you select Datasheet or Tabular. You can also enter data straight into the datasheet instead of depending on a form.

❖ **Title:** Give your form a name after the table you created it in other to recognize it easily in the Navigation pane.

To delete a form, right-click its name in the Navigation pane and select Delete on the shortcut menu.

Entering the data

If you want to unlock a form and start entering data in its database table, show the form's name in the Navigation pane and double-click the form's name. you can also right-click the form and select Open.

To enter data in a form, click the New (Blank) Record button. this button can be found with the Navigation buttons at the base of the form window. A new, empty form displays. Begin typing. Press the Tab key, press the Enter key, or click to navigate from field to field. You can go backward through the fields by pressing Shift+Tab. If you enter the record to some level and you want to start from the beginning, press the Esc key to blank the recent field. Press Esc again to blank all the fields.

Discovery of a Missing Record

Sometimes you might not be able to locate the item or record you need so badly. In case this happens to you, Access provides the Find command. Unlock the database table with the data that requires finding. If you know the field in which the data is positioned, click on the field. Then, on the Home tab, click the Find button.

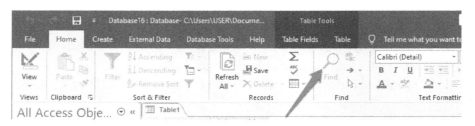

The Find and Replace dialog box appears. See the image below:

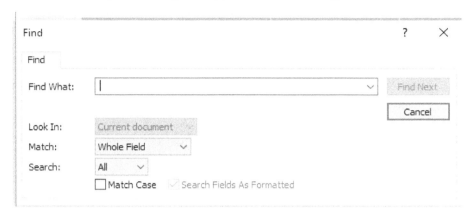

Fill in the dialog box as follows:

- ❖ **Find What:** Enter the item you are looking for in this box.
- ❖ **Look In:** if you click in a field before selecting the Find command, the Resent Field is chosen in this box. Select Current Document on the drop-down menu, to search the whole database table.
- ❖ **Search:** Select an option- All, UP, or Down- that explains the direction to start searching.
- ❖ **Match:** select the option that explains what you know about the item.
- ❖ **Match Case:** choose this check box, if you know the combination of lower and uppercase letters you are after and you enter the combination in the Find What text box.
- ❖ **Search Fields As Formatted:** select this check box if you are searching for a field that has been formatted a particular way, be certain that the number or text you imputed in the Find What text box is formatted appropriately.

Finding and Replacing Data

Finding and replacing data is unusually similar to finding data. The alteration is that you enter data in the Replace With text box as well as the acquainted Find What text box and other option boxes. To find and replace data, kindly follow the steps below:

❖ **Visit the Home tab and click the Replace button**

❖ **After you enter the replacement data in the Replace With text box make sure that the entire Field is chosen in the Match drop-down menu.**

❖ **Conducting a find and replace operation with Any Part of the Field or Start of the Field selected in the Match drop-down menu can have unintended consequences.**

CHAPTER FIVE

Sorting and Filtering for Data

Now that you have laid the foundation, you can put your database through its paces and make it do what databases are meant to do: offer information of one kind or another. This chapter describes how to beleaguer an Access database for names, dates, addresses, statistical averages, and so on. It reveals how to sort records and filter a database table to view records of a certain kind.

Sorting Records in a Database Table

For records to appear in alphabetical, numerical, or date order in one field, you need to sort the records in a database table. You can locate records faster by sorting them in a database. Records can be sorted in ascending or descending order.

Sorting records

Kindly follow the instructions below to sort records in a database table:

❖ **In Datasheet view, click anywhere in the field by which you want to sort the records.**
❖ **Click the Ascending or Descending button, on the Home tab.**

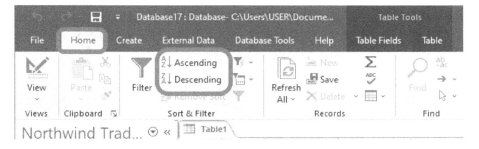

Filtering to discover information

Filtering isolates all the records in a database table that have the same field values or almost the same field values. For all the records in the table to be displayed on the datasheet, only records that meet the filtering criteria are displayed. The fundamental idea behind filtering is to select a field value in the database table and make use of it as the standard for locating or excluding records. For instance, you can find all the orders taken in June or all the orders for a particular customer.

Diverse ways to filter a database table

Below are the four ways to filter a database table. You have to visit the Datasheet view on the Home tab to start filtering operations.

❖ **Filter by Selection:** Select all or aspects of a field in the database table, click the Selection button, and select a filtering option. Access isolates all records with the data you choose.

❖ **Filter by Form:** Click the Advanced button and select Filter by Form. A form appears with one drop-down menu for each field in your table. From the drop-down menu, make selections to define the records you are searching for and click the Toggle Filter button.

❖ **Filter for Input:** Choose the field you want to filter with and click the Filter button. A dialog comes into sight for you to select values in the field.

❖ **Advanced Filter/Sort:** Click the Advanced button and select Advanced Filter/Sort. The Filter window unlocks. Drag the name of the field you want to filter into the grid. Then select a Sort option and enter a search criterion.

Unfiltering a database table

When you are done filtering a database table, apply one of these methods to unfilter it and view all the records in the table again:

❖ Click the word Filtered at the bottom of the window. You can click this word again or click the Toggle Filter button to repeat the filter operation.

❖ On the Home tab, click the Toggle Filter button, you can click this button again to repeat the filter operation.

❖ On the Home tab, click the Advanced button and select Clear All Filters on the drop-down menu.

Filtering by selection

Follow these instructions to filter by selection:

1. **Show the database table that requires filtering in the Datasheet view.**
2. **Inform Access how to filter the records:** to locate all records with the same text or value in a certain field, click in a field with the value or text.
3. **On the Home tab, click the Selection button and select a filtering option.**

Filtering by form

Kindly follow the steps below to filter by form:

1. **In Datasheet view, visit the Home tab, click the Advanced button, and then select Filter by form on the drop-down menu.**

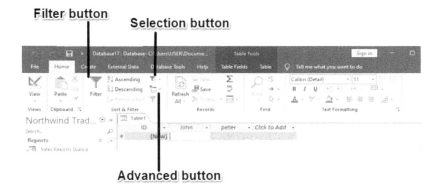

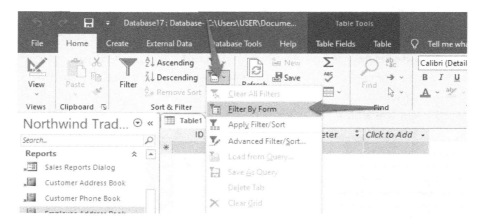

2. **Click in a field, unluck its drop-down menu, and select a value on the drop-down menu or enter a comparison value.**

3. **If you wish, enter more criteria for the filtering operation:** you can impute values in other fields and also filter more than once in the same field.

4. **Click the Toggle Filter button:** The outcomes of the filtering operation are displayed in the datasheet.

Filtering for input

Apply this method to detach records that fall within a numerical or date range. Kindly follow these instructions to filter for input:

1. **Show the database table that you want to filter in Datasheet view.**

2. **Choose the field with the data you want to use for the filter operation:** to choose a field, click its name along the top of the datasheet.

3. **On the Home tab, click the Filter button.**

4. **Inform Access how to filter the database table:** you can select values or describe a data range.

CHAPTER SIX

Querying: The fundamentals

Querying is all about asking questions of a database and obtaining an answer in the form of records that meet the query criteria. You need to query when you want to ask a thorough question of a database. Access provides numerous diverse ways to query a database which will be discussed later in this chapter. The following pages introduce you to queries, how to create them, and how to change them.

Creating a new query

To create a new query, begin on the Create tab and click the Query Wizard button or Query Design.

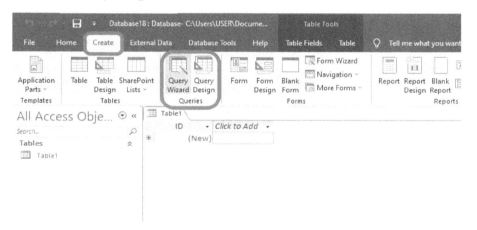

❖ **Create the query with a wizard:** Click the Query Wizard button to reveal the New Query dialog box select a wizard option and answer the questions that the Query Wizard asks.

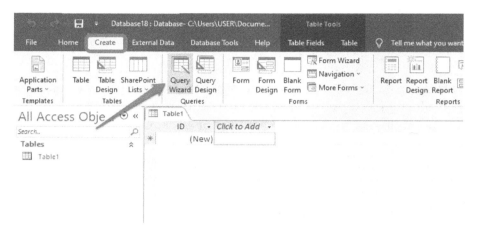

❖ **Create the query in Design view:** Click the Query Design button to view the Query in the Design window, then construct your query in the Design window.

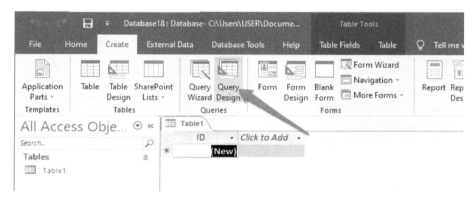

Viewing queries in Design and Datasheet views

Choose a query on the Navigation pane and apply these methods to view it in Datasheet or Design view. The datasheet view displays the outcomes of running a query. Create and change queries in the Design view.

> **Opening in Datasheet view:** On the Navigation pane, double-click the query's name and select Open on the shortcut menu.
> **Opening in Design view:** Right-click the query's name in the Navigation pane and select Design view on the shortcut menu.

Table pane

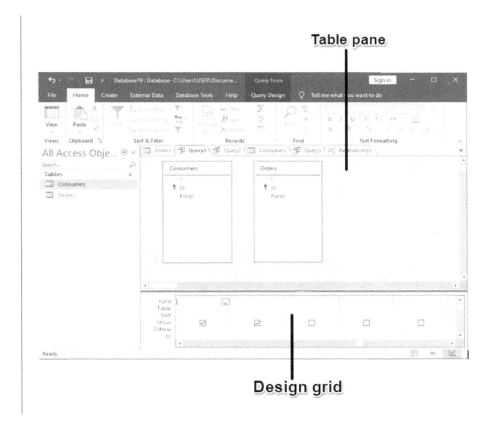

Design grid

> ➢ **Swapping between views on the status bar:** Click the Datasheet View or Design View button on the right-hand side of the status bar.
> ➢ **Swapping between views by right-clicking:** Right-click the query's title bar and select Datasheet View or Design View.
> ➢ **Swapping between views with the view button:** On the Home tab, unlock the drop-down list on the View button. then select Design View or Datasheet View on the drop-down list.

Navigating your way around the Query Design window

The Query Design window is where you create a query or retool a query you created already. Change to Design view to see the Query Design window. This window will appear immediately after you click the Query Design button to create a new query. The Query Design window is separated into halves:

55

> **Table pane:** Lists the database tables you are querying as well as the fields in each table. You can drag the tables to new locations or modify the size of the table by dragging it and seeing more fields.

> **Design grid:** Lists which fields to query from the tables, how to sort the query outcomes, which fields to display in the query results, and criteria for locating records in fields.

Selecting which database tables to query

Kindly follow the instructions below to select which database tables to obtain information from in a query:

❖ **Visit the (Query Tools) Query Design tab and click the Add Tables button.**

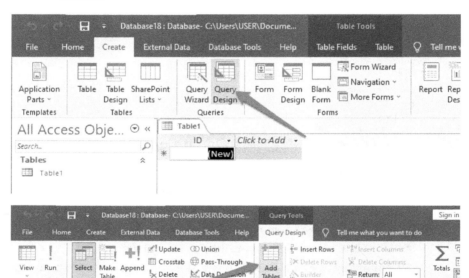

The Add Tables task pane unlocks. It lists all the tables in your database.

❖ **Position the names of tables you want to query in the Table pane**
You can apply these methods to position a table in the Table pane:
  - Double-click a table name in the Add Tables task pane.
  - Drag a table name from the Add Tables task pane to the Table pane.

- Ctrl+click table names to select more than one table, and then drag the table names onto the Table pane.

Click the Add Tables button on the (Query Tools) Query Design tab, If you cannot see the Add Tables task pane.

Selecting which fields to query

Immediately after you have selected which tables to query, the next thing to do is to select which fields to query from the tables you chose. The object is to list fields from the Table pane in the first row of the Design grid. Data from fields listed in the first row of the Design grid is used to produce query results.

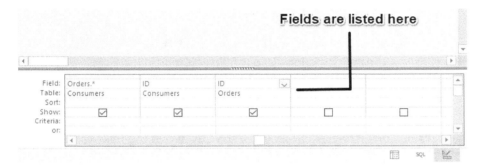

Access provides these methods for listing field names in the first row of the Design grid:

- ❖ **Dragging a field name:** Drag a field name into a column on the Design grid.
- ❖ **Double-clicking a field name:** double-click a field name to position it in the next available column in the Design grid.
- ❖ **Selecting a table and field name:** click in the Table row, unlock the drop-down menu, and select the name of a table. Then in the Field box directly above, unlock the drop-down menu and select a field name.
- ❖ **Choosing all the fields in a table:** In the case you want all the fields from a table to display in the query outcomes, either double-click the asterisk(*) at the top of the list of the field names or drag the asterisk into the Design grid.

57

If you want to remove a field name from the Design grid, choose it and press the Delete key or visit the (Query Tools) Query Design tab and click the Delete Columns button.

Sorting the query outcomes or results

The sorted row of the Design grid below the Table name entails a drop-down menu. To sort the query, click the drop-down menu in a field and select Ascending or Descending to sort the results of a query on a certain field. To sort the outcomes or results on many fields, be certain that the first field to be sorted displays to the left of the other fields. Access reads the sort order from left to right.

MOVING FIELD COLUMNS ON THE QUERY GRID

Kindly follow these instructions to put field columns in the right order in the Query grid:

1. **Click a column's selector button to choose a column.**

   This button is the narrow gray box directly above the field name.

2. **Click the selector button again and drag the column to the left or right.**

Entering criteria for a query

What distinguishes a run-of-the-mill query from a supercharged query is a criterion, an expression you enter on the Criteria line beneath a field. Enter criteria on the Criteria line of the Query grid. By entering criteria, you can locate records in the database with amazing correctness.

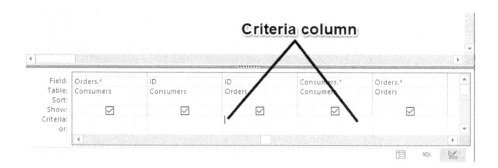

Criteria column

Field:	Orders.*	ID	ID	Consumers.*	Orders.*
Table:	Consumers	Consumers	Orders	Consumer	Orders
Sort:					
Show:	☑	☑	☑	☑	☑
Criteria:					
or:					

When you need assistance writing an expression for a query, try clicking the Builder button to create your query in the Expression Builder dialog box. This button can be found on the (Query Tools) Query Design tab. Some of the Criteria to enter are listed below:

- Numeric criteria
- Text criteria
- Date criteria

Saving and running a query

To save a query and engrave its name forever in the Navigation pane, click the Save button on the Quick Access toolbar and enter a descriptive name in the Save As dialog box. The name you enter displays in the Queries group in the Navigation pane.

After you strenuously create your query, take it for a test drive. To run a query:

➢ **Starting from the Query Design window:** Click the Run button on the (Query Tools) Design tab.
➢ **Starting from the Navigation pane:** Double-click an existing query's name, and select Open on the shortcut menu.

Six kinds of Queries

Access provides a numerous kind of queries but I will only be explaining six of them in this chapter:

❖ **Select Query:** A select query is the standard kind of query, which I discussed earlier in this chapter. It puts together information from one or more database tables and shows the information in a datasheet. It is the most common query and the starting point for most other queries.

❖ **Top-value query:** A top-value query is an easy way to locate, in a Number or Currency field, the lowest or highest values.

❖ **Summary query:** This is the same as a top-value query, it is a way of obtaining collective information about all the data in a field.

❖ **Calculation query:** A calculation query is one in which calculations are performed as an aspect of the query. Follow the steps below to create a calculation query:

- Create a query as you always do and be certain to include the fields you want to use for calculation purposes in the Query grid.

- Impute a name for the Calculation field and follow it with a colon, in the Field box of a blank field.

- After the colon, in square brackets ([]), impute the name of a field whose data you use for the calculation.

- Complete the calculation.

- Click the Run button to run your calculation query.

❖ **Update query:** An update query is a way to reach into a database and update records in numerous diverse tables all at a time. Kindly follow the steps below to run an Update query:

- Visit the Design view, move to the (Query Tools) Query Design tab, and click the Update button.

- In the field with data that requires updating, impute text or a value in the Update To line.

- Click the Run button.

❖ **Delete Query:** A delete query deletes records and does not give you the privilege to obtain the records back if you change your mind about deleting them. Be careful about running delete queries.

CHAPTER SEVEN

Presenting Data in a Report

The best way to present data in a database table or query is to present it in a report. Reports are easy to read and understand. In this chapter, you will learn how to create reports, open them, and edit them.

Creating a Report

The most appropriate way to create a report is to base your report on a query. You can query your database from inside the Report Wizard. The best way is to run a query to produce the results you want in your report, save your query, and then create a report from the query results. How to create a query has been explained in chapter six of this mini-book.

To create a report with the Report Wizard, visit the Create tab and click the Report Wizard button. you notice the first of numerous Report Wizard dialog boxes. Consult the dialog boxes as follows, clicking the Next button as you move along:

- ❖ **Tables/Queries:** Unlock the Table/Queries drop-down menu and select the query where the information in the report will come from. A list of fields in the query is displayed in the Available Field box.
- ❖ **Available Fields and Selected Fields:** Choose the fields whose data you want in the report by choosing the fields one at a time and clicking the >button. by doing this, it moves field names from the Available Fields box to the Selected Fields box. Add all the field names by clicking the >>button.
- ❖ **Do you want to Add Any Grouping Levels?** Add subheadings in your report by selecting a field name and clicking the >button to make it a subheading.
- ❖ **What Sort of Order Do You Want?** Choose up to four fields to sort the data in your report.
- ❖ **How would you like to lay your report?** To select a layout for your report, experiment with the options, and see the Preview box. You may have to print your report in Landscape View if your report has a lot of fields.

- ❖ **What Title Do You Want for Your Report?** Enter a descriptive title. The name you select displays in the Reports group in the Navigation pane.
- ❖ **Preview the Report:** Pick this option button and click Finish.

Below is an example image of a Report.

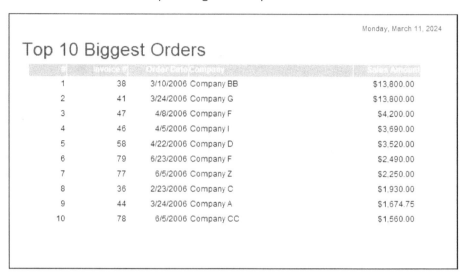

	Invoice #	Order Date	Company	Sales Amount
				Monday, March 11, 2024

Top 10 Biggest Orders

	Invoice #	Order Date	Company	Sales Amount
1	38	3/10/2006	Company BB	$13,800.00
2	41	3/24/2006	Company G	$13,800.00
3	47	4/8/2006	Company F	$4,200.00
4	46	4/5/2006	Company I	$3,690.00
5	58	4/22/2006	Company D	$3,520.00
6	79	6/23/2006	Company F	$2,490.00
7	77	6/5/2006	Company Z	$2,250.00
8	36	2/23/2006	Company C	$1,930.00
9	44	3/24/2006	Company A	$1,674.75
10	78	6/5/2006	Company CC	$1,560.00

Opening and Viewing Reports

Kindly follow the steps below to open a report:

1. **In the Navigation pane, choose the Reports group.**

   You will notice the names of the reports you created.

2. **Double-click a report name or right-click a name and select Open from the shortcut menu.**

   The report is displayed in Report view.

Fine-tuning a Report

Access provides numerous tools for modifying the layout and appearance of a report. In the Report group of the Navigation pane, right-click a report and select Layout View on the shortcut menu. Your report comes into sight in Layout view, as displayed below, in this view, using tools on the (Report Layout Tools) Report Layout Design, Arrange, Format, and Page Setup tabs, you can fine-tune your report's appearance.

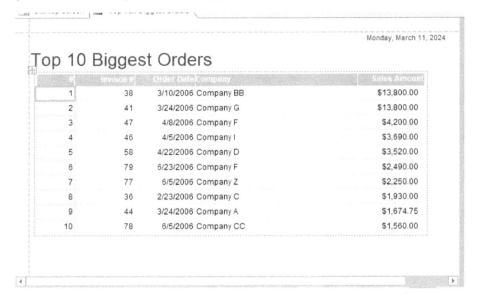

You can modify a report's appearance in Report Layout View without navigating too much trouble if you kindly follow these steps:

- ❖ **Selecting a new layout:** On the (Report Layout Tools) Arrange tab, click the Tabular button and select an option on the drop-down menu, to modify your report's layout.

- ❖ **Including page numbers:** Visit the (Report Layout Tools) Report Layout Design tab and click the Page Numbers button.

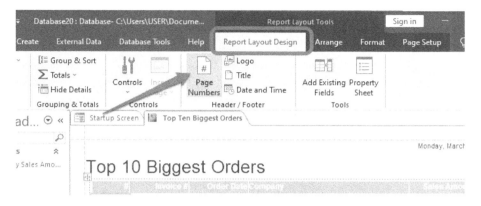

The Page Number dialog box appears, see the image below:

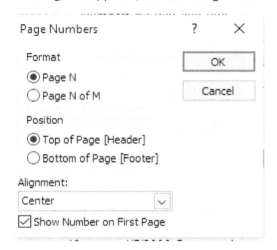

Select the Page N option to show a page number only, or choose the Page N of M option button to show a page number as well as the total number of pages in the report. Select Position and Alignment options to clarify where on the page to place the page number.

❖ **Changing the margins:** On the (Report Layout Tools) Page Setup tab, click the Margins button and pick Normal, Wide, or Narrow on the drop-down list.

CONCLUSION

I believe you now have in-depth knowledge of how to use Microsoft Access 365 after going through every aspect of this book, I am very sure you can now Start Access and navigate your way around the ribbon tab, and I also believe you now know how to Create a database file that you will use to save the database information, and also working with the Access Navigation pane, construction of the database table, Entering fields into each database table, Entering data directly into the table or employ the help of a Form, and many more.

INDEX

A

Access 365 · 4
addresses · 47
Ascending · 56
asterisk · 55

B

bold · 32

C

Calculation query · 58
Close button · 22
confirmation box. · 39
Criteria · 56

D

database · 5
database table · 18, 29
Datasheet View · 23
defense · 25
descriptive name · 30
Design grid · 54
Design view · 22
Design window · 37
dialog box · 20
displayed · 36
displays · 34

E

entering · 7
entering data · 41
equivalent · 6

F

Field Size · 29
field value · 47
Fields box · 43
filtering · 49
Find button. · 44
fine-tune · 62

G

General tab · 35

H

hazardous · 38
history · 32

I

information · 25
instructions · 21
irreplaceable · 5

L

Landscape · 60
Layout View · 62
Lookup · 34

M

Match Case · 45
Microsoft Access · 4

N

Navigation pane · 20
Numeric criteria · 57

O

opening screen · 11
outcomes · 52

P

property · 31

Q

query · 8, 51
Query dialog box · 51

R

Report Wizard · 60
Reports · 60

S

shortcut menu · 41
simultaneously · 40

sorted · 47
status bar. · 53
Summary query · 58

T

table names · 21
Table pane · 55
Tabular. · 44
technique · 32
template · 11
text, numbers, dates · 30
The address book · 6
The building blocks · 18
the relationship · 22
the row selector · 41
Toggle Filter button · 48

U

Update query · 58

V

validation rules · 30

W

Wizard · 33
Wizard button · 42